Specialising in lyrical non-fiction picture books, **Mick Manning** and **Brita Granström** have perfected their unique approach to children's books over fifteen years. Sharing the illustrations between them and mixing words and pictures in all sorts of inventive and delightful ways, they have won many awards, including the Smarties Silver Award and the English Association Award.

Their hilarious book *Yuck!* is featured in Mike Leigh's award-winning film *Happy Go Lucky*. Mick and Brita are married with four young sons. They spend their time between the Scottish borders and a small red house they have built in Sweden.

Their other books for Frances Lincoln include the *Fly on the Wall* series, *Dino Dinners* and *Yuck!*.

For Mandy, Andrew, Katherine, Sarah
and Claire Gray

Mick and Brita would like to thank scientific consultant
Professor Adrian Lister.

First published in Great Britain in 2009 by
Frances Lincoln Children's Books, 4 Torriano Mews,
Torriano Avenue, London NW5 2RZ
www.franceslincoln.com

First paperback published in Great Britain and in the USA in 2011

A catalogue record for this book is available from the British Library.

ISBN 978-1-84780-210-1

Illustrated with watercolour and pencil

Set in Base Twelve and The Sans

Printed in Dongguan, Guangdong, China by Toppan Leefung in July 2010

135798642

Woolly Mammoth

Mick Manning
Brita Granström

FRANCES LINCOLN
CHILDREN'S BOOKS

In association with the
Natural History Museum, London

The woolly mammoth was
a type of mammoth that lived
in Britain, Europe and Asia,
as well as North America
during the last Ice Age.

It had shaggy fur
and a thick layer of fat
to keep it warm.
Its tusks were up to
three metres long and a
male could weigh six tons.

Led by an experienced female,
a mammoth herd may have
migrated between feeding
grounds just like African
elephants and reindeer
still do today.

Look at me!
I'm the shaggiest thing you'll ever see.
Lord of this freezing place,
A chieftain of the elephant race,
A big hairy beastie with a big hairy face.

The tip of a mammoth's trunk worked like a finger and thumb, passing food to its mouth.

It used its tusks like snowploughs to find food: grass, moss, willow, sedge, juniper and wild flowers.

Mammoths lived alongside other herbivores like musk oxen, horses and reindeer.

My massive tusks can push, dig or slice,
As I forage for plants beneath snow and ice.
I'm a veggie warrior with bull-neck power!
Yet my delicate trunk can pick the tiniest flower.
I am a gentle giant.

Large carnivores of the Ice Age included wolves, hyenas, bears and lions.

Ice Age lions preyed on large herbivores – just like African lions do today.

Spotted hyenas live in Africa now – but scientists have found their bones and food remains in caves all over Europe.

A gentle giant . . . really I am!
But if I get angry I become a battering ram
Of tusks and steaming, shaggy hair.
Would I face a hungry wolf, hyena or bear?

Oh yeah!

An undefended mammoth calf would become easy prey.

African elephants and musk oxen form circles for defence. Scientists think mammoths behaved in the same way.

A mammoth's heavy stomping feet could be as dangerous as its tusks!

If danger threatens,
the herd forms a circle,
side-by-side.
Calves in the middle,
our future, our pride.
But if a predator gets inside . . .

What then?
Well, they might get in, stomp
But they never, stomp
Get out again!

A mammoth calf is unbelievably cute.
It thinks life is just a hoot!
Feet sliding! Ears flapping! Trunk feeling,
Trumpeting and squealing!
A mammoth calf is always ready to play.
However bleak dawns the day . . .

Like all baby mammals,
mammoth calves fed on
their mothers' milk.

Mammoths were 'grown up'
at about 15 years old.

In 2007 the 'freeze-dried' body
of a baby mammoth was found
in Siberia. She died about
35,000 years ago – perhaps
by slipping into an icy pool.

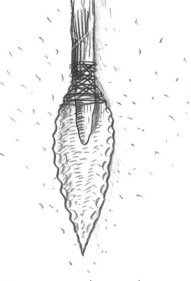

Humans made wooden spears with sharp stone points chipped from flint or another type of hard stone called chert.

This 23,000-year-old 'throwing stick' made of mammoth tusk was found in Poland. Curved to make it spin in the air, it was probably thrown into flocks of birds.

Spear throwers were carved out of tusk, bone or antler to help hunters cast their spear with more power.

When humans hunt us it's a different matter.
Ever hungry, they scream, bash and clatter.
I was once terrified to see
A piece of my sister hunting me!
How? You'll be shocked to hear . . .
She was thrown at me as part of a spear!

In some countries
Scientists have found
piles of mammoth bones
at the bottom of cliffs.
Marks on the bones show that
the meat was cut off by humans.

Were mammoths deliberately
panicked over the edge?
Or did humans scavenge
the meat after
a natural accident?

A pitfall was a clever way
of trapping heavy animals.

'Divide and conquer' is the cunning plan
That lurks deep in the brain of every human.
They split us up, make traps with logs.
Panic us over cliffs or into bogs.
Humans are sneaky, tricky, monkey clever,
But mammoths will never surrender,
Never! Never! Never!

Humans used every bit of a mammoth: meat, offal and fat for food; sinews for sewing and binding; fur and skin for clothes and tents; tusk and bones for carvings, tools and weapons.

Arctic people even today have a special ability called 'the hunters' reflex' which sends extra blood to the hands in freezing temperatures. This prevents numbness and allows delicate fingerwork. So even in the icy cold, human fingers could carve, thread and sew.

Thousands of mammoth ivory beads have been found at Ice Age burial sites in Russia.

To humans we are more than just meat.
To humans a mammoth is a treat.
Every one of us they kill
Gets recycled with craft and skill.
In their hands, our skin and bone
Join forces with wood and stone.

This human face was carved out of mammoth ivory 23, 000 years ago!

In some parts of the Ice Age world, mammoth bones were burned instead of wood for warmth and even used to build shelters.

It's strange that humans feel the need
To burn their food before they feed!
Carried on the icy wind we smell meat and bones,
Roasting over red hot stones!
At night, we hear human fireside chatter.
As we grow thin, they grow fatter!

Ice Age humans carved mammoths in bone, ivory and stone.

They also left behind beautiful cave paintings that show us just how awesome mammoths must have been.

Perhaps cave paintings were a way of thanking the animal spirits and asking them to give good hunting.

We mammoths survive as best we can,
Alongside wolf, bear and hairy human.
But this isn't the sort of place to grow old.
Food is hard. Wind blows cold.
Blizzard cuts like a knife.
Cruel and short is the ice-age life.

One day, maybe I'll be gone without a trace . . .

Mammoths vanished from Britain about 14,000 years ago and became extinct about 4,000 years ago.

Mammoth bodies found in Siberia have been so well preserved by the cold that some still have fur and skin.

North Sea fishing trawlers regularly bring up mammoth bones and teeth. This is because during the Ice Age part of the seabed was dry land.

But until then I'm still chieftain of this frozen place.
A big hairy beastie with a big hairy face.
The shaggiest thing you will never see . . .

Remember me!

Ancestral Mammoth
3 mya–750,000 ya

MYA = MILLION YEARS AGO

Steppe Mammoth
1.7 mya–200,000 ya

Glossary

Animal spirits
Supernatural animal guardians that stone-age peoples still believe bring good or bad luck to hunters.

Carnivore
A meat eater.

Herbivore
A plant eater. Compare with 'Veggie'.

Ice Age
A period in Earth's history when temperatures fell worldwide and more of the Earth's surface was covered in ice.

Ivory
The material that forms the tusks of elephants and other animals.

Mammal
The name for all warm-blooded animals that feed their babies on milk.

Mammoth
A large, extinct sort of elephant that was covered in thick shaggy hair.

Mammoth calf
A baby mammoth.

Columbian Mammoth
1.5 mya–10,000 ya

Woolly Mammoth
700,000 ya–4,000 ya

North Sea

The area of sea between England, Denmark and Holland covers a land where Mammoths once roamed. Scientists call it Doggerland.

Pitfall trap

A deep pit that has been dug out, filled with sharp stakes and covered with branches that are meant to break if a heavy animal walks across them.

Siberia

A vast area of eastern Russia where some of the land is permanently frozen.

Stone Age

Before humans discovered metal, they used stone, bone, antler, tusk and wood to make their tools. The Stone Age is divided into many time periods and lasted for millions of years. There are still some Stone-Age peoples living in the world today, in the Amazon rainforest for example.

Throwing stick

Used for hunting. The boomerang is an Australian throwing stick that will even spin back to its thrower.

Veggie

Vegetarian. An animal that doesn't eat meat. Compare with 'Herbivore'.